JAMAICA

MAJOR WORLD NATIONS
JAMAICA

Frances Wilkins

CHELSEA HOUSE PUBLISHERS
Philadelphia

Chelsea House Publishers

3 5 7 9 8 6 4 2

Library of Congress Cataloging-in-Publication Data

Wilkins, Frances.
Jamaica / Frances Wilkins
p. cm. — (Major world nations)
Includes index.
Summary: Explores the people, history, culture, land, climate, and economy of Jamaica,
one of the group of West Indies islands discovered and named by Christopher
Columbus in 1494.
ISBN 0-7910-4978-7
1. Jamaica—Juvenile literature. [1. Jamaica.] I. Title.
II. Series.
F1868.2.W66   1998
972.92—dc21   98-6897
CIP
AC

ACKNOWLEDGEMENTS

The Author and Publishers are grateful to the following organizations and individuals
for permission to reproduce copyright illustrations in this book:
Ann Bolt; Hutchison Photo Library; Jamaica Tourist Board; The Mansell Collection
Ltd; Spectrum Colour Library; Travel Photo International; Vidocq Photo Library.

CONTENTS

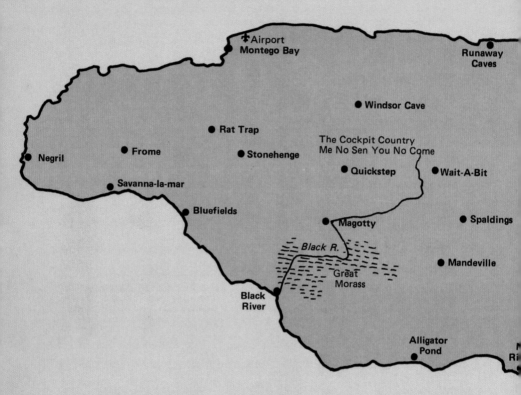

Airport
Montego Bay

Runaway
Caves

● Windsor Cave

● Rat Trap

● Negril

● Frome

● Stonehenge

The Cockpit Country
Me No Sen You No Come

● Quickstep

● Wait-A-Bit

● Savanna-la-mar

● Bluefields

● Magotty

● Spaldings

Black R.

● Mandeville

Great
Morass

Black
River

Alligator
Pond

Ri

FLORIDA
(U.S.A.)

BAHAMAS

DOMINICAN
REPUBLIC

CUBA

PUERTO
RICO

HAITI

GREATER
ANTILLES

HISPANIOLA

LEEWARD
ISLANDS

JAMAICA

WINDWARD
ISLANDS

COLOMBIA

VENEZUELA

CARIBBEAN   SEA

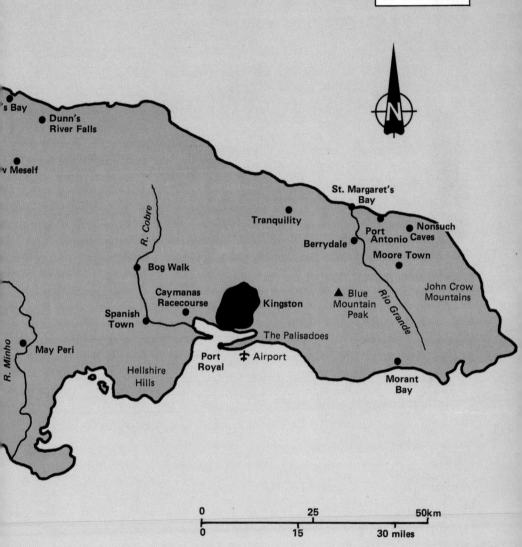

FACTS AT A GLANCE

Land and People

Official Name	Jamaica
Location	Island in the Caribbean Sea; 90 miles south of Cuba and 100 miles west of Haiti
Area	4,411 square miles
Climate	Tropical; mean temperature in the winter is 75 degrees Fahrenheit and in the summer is 80 degrees Fahrenheit
Capital	Kingston
Other Cities	Spanish Town, Portmore, Montego Bay, May Pen
Population	2.5 million
Population Density	570 persons per square mile
Major Rivers	Black, Rio Grande, Martha Brae, White
Mountains	Blue Mountain Range, Port Royal Range
Highest Point	Blue Mountain Peak (7,402 feet)

Official Language	English
Other Languages	Jamaican Patois
Ethnic Groups	Black, East Indian
Religions	Protestant, Baptist, Roman Catholic
Literacy Rate	73 percent

Economy

Natural Resources	Bauxite, gypsum, silica, limestone
Agricultural Products	Sugar, bananas, yams, coconuts, citrus fruits
Industries	Tourism
Major Exports	Rum, marijuana, tobacco, chemicals, food
Currency	Jamaican dollar

Government

Form of Government	Constitutional monarchy with two legislative houses
Government Bodies	Senate and House of Representatives
Formal Head of State	British monarch, who is represented by a Governor-General
Head of Government	Prime Minister
Voting Rights	All Jamaicans over the age of 18 have the right to vote

HISTORY AT A GLANCE

800   The Arawak people, originally from coastal Venezuela and Brazil, arrive in the area.

1494   Columbus lands in Jamaica during his second voyage, on May 5.

1503   Columbus returns to Jamaica on his fourth voyage. He and his crew are marooned for nearly a year. He returns to Spain in ill health and dies in 1506.

1510   Diego Columbus, son of the explorer, leads the first group of Spanish colonists. After several attempts they build a permanent settlement at Villa de la Vega, later known as Spanish Town.

1517   Forced labor and European diseases soon wipe out most of the native people. African slaves are brought in to work for the Spanish. Their descendants will eventually make up 95 percent of the population.

1655   Oliver Cromwell sends an expedition which eventually conquers Jamaica, bringing it permanently under English rule.

1670	Spain formally cedes Jamaica to England as part of the Treaty of Madrid. Spanish Town becomes capital of the province.
1688	Henry Morgan, greatest of the English pirates, dies in retirement as a respectable landowner. The pirates of this era are supported by Britain and mainly attack Spanish ships and colonies.
1713	Britain, France and Spain end a European war by signing the Treaty of Utrecht. Under the treaty Britain receives the *asiento*, or monopoly on the slave trade in the West Indies. Jamaica becomes the center of the English slave trade.
1720	Mary Read and Anne Bonney, the two most famous female pirates, are captured by British authorities near Negril. The pirates of this era are mostly outlaws, operating without government approval.
1729	The Maroon War. The Maroons are escaped slaves who live in the mountains and forests.
1760	Tacky's Rebellion, a well-organized slave revolt, spreads throughout the island. Tacky and his followers are eventually defeated by the British, assisted by the Maroons.
1795	A second Maroon War breaks out. The British eventually agree to let the Maroons return to their free status.
1815	Having been defeated by the Spanish in Venezuela, Simon Bolivar seeks refuge in Jamaica. He remains in exile until the end of 1816, writing his famous "Letter from Jamaica" (*Carta de Jamaica*).

1831 A slave revolt, the Christmas Rebellion, breaks out at Montego Bay under Sam Sharpe. Sam Sharpe (now a national hero) and hundreds of his followers are eventually executed. Criticism of slavery becomes widespread in Great Britain.

1834 Slavery abolished in the British Empire, although most Jamaican slaves must work another four years to compensate their former owners.

1865 The Morant Bay revolt of freed slaves against the local government. The revolt is cruelly suppressed. Britain steps in, removes the local rulers, and turns Jamaica into a Crown Colony, which will be ruled directly from London.

1872 As part of a series of reforms, Kingston replaces Spanish Town as capital of the colony.

1887 Marcus Garvey born in St. Ann's parish, near Ocho Rios. He founds an important Black consciousness movement in the United States and Jamaica. Dying in exile in London in 1940, he is later buried in Jamaica and considered a national hero.

1944 Britain grants Jamaica a new constitution which retains a London-appointed governor, but allows free elections for the local legislature.

1958 The British form the Federation of the West Indies, made up of its territories in the Caribbean.

1959 Jamaica gains full control of its internal affairs, with Britain retaining only a ceremonial governor-general. Free elections are held for all offices and Norman Manley becomes the first prime minister.

1961 After a nationwide referendum, Jamaica withdraws from the Federation of the West Indies.

1962 Jamaica gains full independence, but remains part of the British Commonwealth, with its monarch technically head of state.

1963 The James Bond film *Dr. No* brings other motion picture projects to Jamaica. The Bond books had all been written at Ian Fleming's estate, Goldeneye, near Kingston.

1972 Michael Manley, son of Norman Manley, becomes prime minister.

1980 Violent electoral campaign in which hundreds die. Edward Seaga eventually wins. He is pro-U.S. and the country receives substantial financial aid. The economy is stabilized, but at the cost of reduced wages and benefits for poorer people.

1981 Death of musician Bob Marley at age 36. He had made *reggae*, a form of music rising from the Rastafarian movement, internationally famous.

1989 Popular discontent with Seaga leads to Michael Manley being returned to office.

1992 Manley resigns due to ill health. He is succeeded by his former deputy Percival James Patterson, who becomes the nation's first black prime minister.

1

The Land and the People

The name Jamaica means the "Land of Woods and Water" but to the one and a half million or more visitors who go there every year, it is a land of blue skies and golden sand. Apart from a short rainy season in May and June and another in October, the sun shines all the year round, and there are 200 miles (320 kilometers) of fine, sandy beaches.

Jamaica is one of a group of islands, just off the coast of Central America, called the West Indies. They were given this name by Christopher Columbus, who discovered them in 1494. Columbus knew that the world was round. When he arrived at the islands, he thought he had managed to reach India by sailing west instead of east.

There are several hundred islands in the West Indies. The largest is Cuba, the second largest Hispaniola (divided between Haiti and the Dominican Republic) and the third largest Jamaica. These three

Fine sandy beaches such as this are the major attraction for the thousands of people who visit Jamaica every year.

islands, together with a number of much smaller ones, are called the Greater Antilles, and lie in the part of the Atlantic Ocean which is known as the Caribbean Sea. (For this reason they are often called the Caribbean Islands.)

Jamaica itself covers nearly 4,411 square miles (11,000 square kilometers). It is approximately 140 miles (230 kilometers) from east to west, and varies between 50 miles (80 kilometers) and 22 miles (36 kilometers) from north to south. There is a narrow coastal plain in the south, and lowlands stretch across the west end of the island, but more than half the island is mountainous. The main range runs

A view of the famous Blue Mountains, the great ridge which dominates the eastern end of Jamaica.

from east to west, and mostly varies from about 1,000 feet (300 meters) to 5,000 feet (1,500 meters) above sea level. The highest part of all is the Blue Mountain Peak, in the east of the island, which is almost 7,500 feet (2,300 meters) above sea level, and always seems to be lost in a bluish mist.

The first inhabitants of Jamaica are believed to have been the Ciboneys. They probably came from present-day Florida, but little or nothing is known about them. The first people of whom there is definite trace are the Arawaks, who are thought to have settled in Jamaica around A.D. 800. The Arawaks were a cinnamon-colored people, who probably paddled their way to Jamaica in dugout canoes from the Orinoco region of South America. Unfortunately, little is known about them, except that they were a peaceful community who spent most of their time hunting, fishing and doing a small amount of farming.

Then, in 1494, Christopher Columbus arrived on the island. The Arawaks had no means of defending themselves, and Columbus quickly overcame any resistance. Jamaica was not handed over to any of the great European countries, however. It remained a personal possession of Columbus himself, and of his descendants after his death.

The next major turning-point in Jamaica's history came in 1655. This was the year in which the British arrived, and claimed it as a colony. From then on, most of the island was divided up among absentee British landowners. These landowners often made vast fortunes from the tobacco and cotton grown by the black slaves who had been taken to the West Indies from Africa.

During the early eighteenth century, there was considerable unrest in Jamaica. This only ended with the abolition of slavery in 1834. Trouble broke out again shortly before the Second World War, when the Jamaicans began agitating for independence—just as people were doing in many other British colonies at that time.

Finally, in 1962, Jamaica became an independent country within the Commonwealth. Today, the Head of State is the British Queen, who is represented by a Governor-General. The duties of the

King's House in Kingston, the official residence of the Governor-General. Jamaica is now an independent country within the Common-wealth and the duties of the Governor-General are mainly ceremonial.

Governor-General are mainly ceremonial, however, and the effective head of Jamaica's government is the prime minister.

Like Britain, Jamaica has two Houses of Parliament. There is the Senate, with twenty-one members who are appointed by the Governor-General. Then there is the House of Representatives, with sixty members elected for a term of not more than five years by the votes of all the adults—both men and women—on the island.

The population of Jamaica today is about two and a half million. Of these, about ninety-five percent are either of African, or a mixture of African and European, descent. This means that their

18

skins vary in color from shiny black to brown or sometimes even light coffee-color. The remaining five percent of the population are mainly of European descent, although there are also a certain number of Indians and Chinese.

After years of British rule, the official language of Jamaica is naturally English. But many people in the country districts speak a local *patois* called Creole. Similarly, the vast majority of Jamaicans are Christians, most of them Anglicans (Episcopalians), although there is also a large community of Rastafarians. In addition, there are smaller groups of Jews, Hindus and Muslims.

The economy of Jamaica is based largely on agriculture. One of

An old woman and her grandchild. About ninety-five percent of Jamaicans are of African, or a mixture of African and European, descent.

the major foreign currency earners is sugar, with molasses and rum as important by-products. In recent years, however, the production of sugar has been steadily falling, while cocoa and coffee-production have been steadily rising. Jamaica's most important foreign currency earner is now tourism. In 1994, 1.6 million tourists visited Jamaica, the majority of them from the United States. Other important industries are the production of bauxite and aluminum, cement, tobacco and a number of other consumer goods, which are mostly exported to the United States, Canada and Britain.

The capital of Jamaica is Kingston, which is also its principal port. Kingston lies on the coast at the southeastern end of the island. The second largest town is Montego Bay, which is also the second largest port. It lies in the northwestern part of the island. Jamaica is well-covered with roads linking all the towns and villages. There is also

A mounted policeman in Kingston. Jamaica has an armed police force of about six thousand men.

a railway from Kingston to Montego Bay, a distance of approximately 110 miles (180 kilometers). There are two international airports, one at either end of the island, which are used not only by Jamaica's own airline, but by numerous other international airlines as well.

To maintain law and order, Jamaica has an armed police force of about six thousand men. It also has a regular army of approximately three thousand well-trained soldiers. It has a navy of over one hundred and forty men, chiefly engaged in combating smuggling, and a very small air force of about eighty men.

2

Early History

Christopher Columbus first saw Jamaica in 1494, on his second voyage to the New World. He was so impressed by it that he called it "the fairest island that eyes have ever beheld." During his fourth voyage (1502-3), he and his crew were marooned for a year at present-day St. Ann's Bay, after his ship had run aground. It was during this period that a priest who was with Columbus wrote an account of the Arawaks.

At this time, there were still about 60,000 Arawaks in Jamaica. They lived in small villages of round, thatched huts, mostly in the hilly areas near the coast. They mainly ate shellfish, lizards and coneys (animals rather like large rats), along with bread made from cassava roots; and they liked to smoke tobacco.

The Arawaks put up no opposition when the Spaniards arrived on the island. Apparently it never occurred to them that the Spaniards might be a threat. However, within a hundred years or so the Arawaks had completely disappeared–either because the Spaniards had killed them, or because they had fallen victim to one of the numerous diseases, such as smallpox, which the Spaniards had brought with them. Nevertheless, the Arawaks did not die out leaving no trace. In fact, considerable numbers of their pots, little stone gods and primitive rock carvings have been found. They also left a number of words which have now become part of the English language, including tobacco, potato, hurricane, canoe, hammock, maize, barbecue and cannibal, as well as the word Xamayaca (or Jamaica) itself.

In 1510, Diego Columbus (Christopher's son) founded a settlement near present-day St. Ann's Bay. He called it *Sevilla Nueva*, or New Seville, after the famous city in Spain. It was not a healthy site, however, and just over twenty years later the Spaniards moved their capital to Villa de la Vega, meaning "the town on the plain," which is known today as Spanish Town. For a time, Villa de la Vega was easily the largest town on the island. Although it was some distance inland, up the River Cobre, it was also quite an important port. It was a convenient place for ships plying between Spain and the New World (particularly Mexico and Peru) to drop anchor for a couple of days, to have a rest and take on fresh supplies of food.

It was about this time that the first Africans arrived in Jamaica. With the disappearance of the Arawaks, the Spaniards found that they were short of people to do the heavier type of manual work for them. So they imported slaves from Africa.

The arrival of the British in Jamaica happened almost by accident. Oliver Cromwell, who was a Protestant, wanted to wrest control of the Caribbean from the Catholic Spaniards. So he sent an expedition under the joint command of Admiral Sir William Penn and General Robert Venables to capture the island of Hispaniola (now Haiti and the Dominican Republic). However, the expedition was heavily defeated, losing a third of its forces. To try to make up for this disaster, the British decided to attack Jamaica instead. The remaining force of nearly five thousand men sailed into Kingston Harbor on May 10, 1655 and, in return for a safe passage for Spanish settlers to Cuba and Hispaniola, the governor of Villa de la Vega surrendered.

In 1670 an official peace treaty, called the Treaty of Madrid, was signed. But a small number of Spaniards and freed Blacks still continued a guerilla war in the mountains. These "Maroons," as they were called (meaning "wild men of the mountains" in Spanish) went on resisting for several generations, and made peace with the British only in 1739, on the understanding that they should retain a certain measure of independence.

It was about the time that the British arrived in Jamaica that the Caribbean became the haunt of pirates and smugglers. These were of many nationalities and would attack any ship which they thought was carrying a valuable cargo. Officially, of course, all the European countries condemned this behavior, but most of the governments seemed willing to turn a blind eye to such activities when it suited them. For example, one English pirate named Henry Morgan was in trouble with the British authorities for attacking Spanish ships. But only a few years later he was given a knighthood and appointed as Governor of Jamaica. From then onwards, Morgan did his best to

Maroons re-enacting their struggles against the British in the late seventeenth and early eighteenth centuries.

put an end to piracy around Jamaica, and even sent some of his old pirate friends to the gallows.

Despite Henry Morgan's efforts, however, piracy continued to flourish. Port Royal (just outside Kingston) had so many pirates and smugglers that it was nicknamed "the wickedest city in the world." Then, on June 7, 1692, Port Royal was hit by a terrible natural disaster. There was a tremendous earthquake, during which two-thirds of the city suddenly slid into the sea. Over two thousand people are believed to have died. In addition, a thousand houses, as

The tombstone of Lewis Galdy, in Port Royal churchyard, which tells us that Galdy ". . . was swallowed up in the great earthquake in the year 1692 and by the providence of God was by another shock thrown into the sea and miraculously saved by swimming until a boat took him up."

well as several churches and a prison, disappeared beneath the waves. This was followed in the next few years by a series of fires and hurricanes, which people said were a punishment on the wicked city from God, and this belief gradually helped to bring piracy to an end in the Caribbean.

Meanwhile, legitimate trade had been steadily increasing in Jamaica. In fact, ever since the days of the Spaniards Jamaica had sent a small, but steady, amount of agricultural produce abroad. With its extremely fertile soil and its hot, moist climate almost any type of crop would flourish, from cacao (used in the making of cocoa) to indigo, wheat and tobacco.

It was sugar that was by far the most profitable crop, however. This had been introduced into Jamaica by Christopher Columbus, who had taken some sugarcane seedlings there from Spain. Then, with the arrival of the British in the late seventeenth century, the sugar industry had grown dramatically, and quickly dominated the island's entire economy.

The only drawback to growing sugarcane was that it needed a huge labor force. What was more, the work was extremely heavy and unpleasant, especially under the burning Jamaican sun. The British sugar plantation owners' solution to the problem of finding strong, cheap labor was to import vast numbers of slaves from Africa.

3

Sugar and Slaves

There had always been slaves in Jamaica from the time when the Spaniards had ruled the island. But it was not until the sugar industry began to expand in the early eighteenth century that the trickle of slaves suddenly turned into a flood. In fact, the slave traders just could not bring the slaves to Jamaica fast enough, and by 1785 the country had no less than a quarter of a million of them, outnumbering the white population by nearly fifteen to one.

Almost from the outset, the slave trade was a three-sided affair. Ships left Britain with cheap goods to barter for slaves in West Africa, and then shipped them across the Atlantic to the West Indies. There, in exchange for the slaves, the ships took on board local produce such as sugar, rum or tobacco, and headed back across the Atlantic to Britain.

The conditions under which the slaves were taken to Jamaica were almost indescribable. First, the slaves were chained hand and foot, and branded with the trader's mark, like cattle. Then they were herded into the holds of the ships where, with no sanitation

An engraving of a slave ship, showing the atrocious conditions and treatment to which the slaves were subjected.

and very little ventilation, many of them died long before the terrible voyage was over. When they arrived in Jamaica, conditions were usually no better. The slaves were crowded into comfortless compounds, or pens, while they were waiting to be sold. Then, husbands separated from wives and children from their parents, they were sold and taken away to the sugar plantations.

The majority of slaves were formed into gangs to work in the fields. They did the heavy and unpleasant tasks such as preparing the earth before the cane was planted, and then cutting the cane and bundling it up at harvesttime. Other slaves worked in the factories, grinding the cane, boiling the sugar and filling the heavy barrels in which the sugar was to be sent overseas. Luckier slaves became

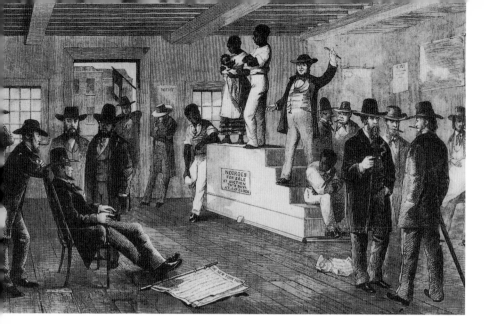

A slave auction in the New World. The unfortunate slaves were usually treated more like animals than people.

servants in the grand houses of the landowners. Some were treated kindly, and eventually became valued family retainers. Others who showed special aptitudes were taught skills such as carpentry or masonry by craftsmen specially brought out from Britain, and examples of their excellent work still exist.

By and large, however, the slaves were unhappy and resentful. As they outnumbered the white people on such a massive scale, they began to pose a real threat. This did not bother the wealthy absentee British landowners too much, but it was a constant worry to the British managers and overseers who were actually in charge of the slaves. There were numerous revolts among the slaves throughout the eighteenth and early nineteenth centuries—far more in Jamaica,

30

in fact, than in any other part of the West Indies. The revolts were always suppressed, however, and were inevitably followed by the most horrible and inhuman punishments which the British overseers were able to devise.

By the beginning of the nineteenth century, the slaves were determined to obtain their freedom. At first they had little support in their struggle, except from a small number of nonconformist ministers. Most of these ministers soon found their churches and even their homes burnt down, as the powerful landowners, and even the Jamaican government itself, did everything possible to silence any opposition to slavery.

Public feeling in Britain, however, was gradually being awakened. Preachers like William Wilberforce from Hull were keeping up a constant battle to bring the situation to people's attention. More and more people in Britain, especially those with strong religious views, began to denounce the slave trade, saying that everyone had a God-given right to be free.

As a result, in 1834, the British parliament brought in a law abolishing slavery. This said that every slave in every part of the British Empire should be given his freedom immediately. The Jamaican government gave the aggrieved landowners a small amount of compensation, amounting to approximately 27 British pounds for every adult slave, and 4 British pounds for every child slave they possessed. In addition, the government did its best to try to safeguard the sugar industry. It said that all the ex-slaves must continue working for their previous owners for a small salary for at least a further three years. After this most of the ex-slaves left the plantations, and tried to obtain small pieces of land of their own. Ironically, many of them suffered far greater hardship when they had been freed than they had ever done when they were slaves.

By 1865, the former slaves could stand it no longer. So a man named Paul Bogle led a band of them to the courthouse at Morant Bay in a last desperate attempt to gain justice. The government troops refused to let them enter, however, and in the ensuing struggle the courthouse was burnt down and sixteen of the government's supporters were killed. Reprisals were swift and unbelievably harsh. Nearly four hundred and fifty of the ex-slaves, including Paul Bogle, were either shot or hanged. When news of their execution reached Britain, the British government sent a protest against the inhumanity of the punishment and dismissed the

A descendant of the slaves sent from Africa to work on Jamaica's sugar plantations.

island's governor; and in 1866 Jamaica was given the status of a British Crown Colony.

Towards the end of the nineteenth century, the new banana trade improved the plight of the black people a little more. But as late as the 1930s, Jamaica was still a country with thousands of poverty-stricken Blacks ruled by a few wealthy Whites. In 1938, there were widespread riots, as a protest against the very low wages paid to the Blacks, and the lack of even a vote by which they could make known their views.

Two black Jamaicans then came to prominence. One was Alexander Bustamente, an important trade unionist, and the other was Norman Washington Manley, a barrister. Although they were cousins, they were great rivals. Both became national heroes for the unremitting efforts they made to gain Jamaica's freedom.

Eventually, in 1944, the British drew up a new constitution for Jamaica. This gave a vote to every adult, which increased the number of people on the electoral register nearly thirty-three times. On August 6, 1962, Jamaica became fully independent, although it continues to have a Governor-General representing the British crown, and it still remains a part of the Commonwealth of Britain.

4

Religions and Cults

The majority of Jamaicans belong to the Church of England. In this respect, Jamaica differs from most of the other West Indian islands, which are mainly Roman Catholic. There are, however, considerable numbers of Roman Catholics in Jamaica, as well as Baptists and Methodists, and smaller numbers of almost every other well-known Christian denomination.

The first Christian church to be built in Jamaica was Roman Catholic. It was erected by the Spaniards at Sevilla Nueva (near present-day St. Ann's Bay) in 1525. During the next one hundred and thirty years, many other Catholic churches were founded by the Spaniards, in various parts of the island, but none of them still remains standing today.

Catholicism was banned when the British captured Jamaica in 1655. Everyone was forced to belong to the Church of England, which was one reason why most of the Spaniards decided to leave the island. In fact, it was not until 1792 that any other Christian denomination was permitted; and, until 1865, the Anglican Church was supported out of the taxes.

Once other Christian denominations were allowed, all kinds of different missionaries began arriving in Jamaica. These included quite a number of Baptists, as well as smaller numbers of Roman Catholics and Methodists. They all opened churches or chapels, and sometimes schools, but none of them managed to become a serious rival to the Church of England on the island.

Nevertheless, the Church of England did lose the support of some of the slaves. This was because it did nothing to help the slaves' fight for freedom, as most of the rich landowners were supporters of the Church. But ministers of various Free Churches (particularly the Baptists) were often great champions of the slaves, and a certain number of the slaves naturally decided to join these denominations.

The earliest non-Christian group of settlers in Jamaica were the Jews. They left Spain and Portugal when the Jews were persecuted there in the sixteenth century. Nowadays they still tend to be a rather self-contained group, who practice their religion in exactly the same way as Jews do in every other part of the world.

A much newer group of settlers are the Hindus and Muslims. There are approximately thirty to forty thousand of them in Jamaica, and their families all came originally from India. They are, in fact, the descendants of thousands of Indian farmworkers, who were persuaded to settle in Jamaica by the British government in the 1860s and 1870s to work on the sugar plantations.

Alongside all these well-recognized religions, there are numerous other cults and persuasions in Jamaica. Some of these are based

An Anglican church in rural Jamaica. Most Jamaicans are Anglicans—a legacy of British rule of the island.

rather loosely on Christianity, but differ widely from the usually accepted forms of belief. Others were brought over from Africa by the early slaves, and have survived all efforts by both Spanish and British missionaries to stamp them out.

Most of these primitive cults are generally grouped together and called Pocomania. (This is sometimes said to come from the Spanish, and to mean "a little madness.") Each group varies slightly in its beliefs, but they all seem to combine certain simple Christian teachings with very ancient West African superstitions and practices. Pocomanians believe that everyone has a soul, which goes to either heaven or hell after death. But they also believe that everyone has a ghost (or "duppy"), which remains on earth forever. Their chief form of worship is to go into a trance, when they believe that spirits take over their bodies and make them sing, dance and prophesy the future; and they also believe that these spirits can cure them of illness.

One of the old West African cults found in Jamaica is called Obeah. This is really a kind of black magic, and the "obeah man" is little more than a witch doctor. Officially, Obeah is illegal in Jamaica, but almost every town and village has at least one obeah man, or perhaps obeah woman. The obeah men are believed to possess all kinds of weird and wonderful powers. For example, they claim they can protect people from illness, from being cheated or robbed and, of course, from spells cast by any other obeah men! They sell "love oils," to ensure that people do not lose their boyfriends or girlfriends, and even "keep-your-job oils" to protect the user against unemployment!

One of the best known sects in Jamaica today is quite modern, however. This is the Rastafarian movement, which was founded in 1930 by a black American named Marcus Garvey. The Rastafarians revere Emperor Haile Selassie I of Ethiopia (whose name before he became emperor was Ras Tafari), as they believe that he was the direct descendant of King Solomon and the Queen of Sheba. (Selassie died in 1975.)

There are about seventy thousand Rastafarians in Jamaica today. They are all Blacks, and are easily recognizable by their "dreadlocks" (long frizzy hair). Their motto is "Peace and Love,"

A Pocomania temple in Kingston. Pocomania draws heavily on Christian rites for its music and doctrine, but has a thread of African culture running through its beliefs and ceremonies.

and on the whole they appear to live reasonably happy lives in Jamaica, although their ultimate aim is supposed to be to settle in Ethiopia.

In recent years, the Rastafarians have become well-known for their music. This is called *reggae*, and it often has lyrics containing a Rastafarian religious message. The singer Bob Marley made *reggae* music popular all over the world, especially among young people, who like its incredible vitality, and its strong, positive beat.

Curious as it may seem, Jamaicans quite often follow more than one religious belief. Although they may officially be Christian, they may also quite openly practice some totally different religion. For

38

example, it is not at all uncommon for Jamaicans to go to church on a Sunday after having spent all Saturday evening ridding themselves of evil spirits to the beat of drums.

Nevertheless, despite all these odd practices, one thing is certain. Nearly all Jamaicans have some kind of religious faith, and many of them are extremely devout. Churches and temples are always full on Sundays and other holy days with crowds of enthusiastic worshippers from every section of society.

5

Kingston and Port Royal

Kingston was founded in the late seventeenth century. It was founded after a serious earthquake had caused much of Port Royal, which had previously been the largest town in the area, to slip down into the sea. However, Kingston did not become the capital of the island until 1872, when the seat of government was transferred there from the previous capital, Spanish Town.

Today Kingston's population is growing very rapidly. It was only half a million in 1970, but it is now about three-quarters of a million. This is partly due to the very high birth rate, and partly to the continuous influx of people from the country districts who arrive looking for work. There are also many different types of people living in Kingston. As well as Africans, Europeans, Jews and Asians, there are large numbers who are a mixture of races. In addition, there are great contrasts in the people's way of life, from that of the wealthy businessmen, to that of the countless ragged beggars with nowhere to sleep but the streets.

Unfortunately, Kingston is not an attractive city. Although it has a beautiful setting, the buildings are a jumble of styles. In fact, no one but the Spaniards, who laid out the streets on a gridiron pattern, seems to have made any effort to plan the city, and this has had disastrous results.

Architecturally, Kingston falls into two sections. First, there is Old Kingston, where it is still possible to trace the plan of the city as it was laid out by the Spaniards. Most of this area is now a mass of overcrowded shanty buildings, with dirt roads, where pigs, goats and starving mongrel dogs always seem to be roaming.

Nevertheless, there are a few interesting buildings in Old Kingston. One of these is the Institute of Jamaica, which houses, among other treasures, what are known as the "Shark Papers." The

A shack in Kingston made of old scrap iron. Many of Kingston's inhabitants live in great poverty.

An aerial view of the bustling port of Kingston, capital of Jamaica—the seventh largest natural harbor in the world.

"Shark Papers" are the log of a smuggling vessel called the *Nancy*. In 1799, when the smugglers saw a customs' ship, the log was thrown overboard and later discovered in the belly of a shark.

Also in Old Kingston is Jamaica's biggest and liveliest market. This is called the Coronation Market, and is always a bustling maze of stalls–particularly on Fridays and Saturdays. Market women, known as *higglers* (hagglers), travel to Kingston with their produce from all the surrounding towns and villages; and virtually anything grown or produced locally can be bought there.

The other section of the city, called New Kingston, was laid out

42

after a terrible earthquake in 1907. Most of it is on the slightly higher ground which runs into the foothills of the Blue Mountains. Many of Kingston's wealthier people live here in large, well-maintained bungalows. Some of the city's loveliest old buildings, which managed to withstand the 1907 earthquake, are also found in this area.

The elegant old buildings are mostly constructed in the old colonial style. This means they are built of wood, with wide balconies at the front. They are usually set in beautiful gardens, with massive tropical trees and shrubs such as rhododendrons, which produce large, colorful flowers.

One of the finest old buildings is Devon House, in Hope Road, which now houses the National Gallery of Art. It was built in 1881, by one of the first black millionaires in Jamaica. Like most of Jamaica's old homes, it is supposed to be haunted by a duppy—in this case a beautiful girl, who is seen from time to time combing her long, blond hair, in one of the upper rooms.

King's House, the residence of the Governor-General, is also in Hope Road. A few streets away, in Montrose Road, is Vale Royal, the residence of the Prime Minister. Vale Royal is an eighteenth-century house, which was originally surrounded by a plantation. It still has the lookout tower from which ships entering and leaving the harbor could be observed.

At the extreme eastern end of Hope Road are the Royal Botanical Gardens (commonly known as the Hope Gardens). The gardens cover two hundred acres (ninety hectares), and are easily the largest in the Caribbean. From there it is only a short walk to the foot of

Devon House, which now houses the National Gallery of Art.

the Long Mountain, which runs north to south along the eastern side of the city, and rises at one point to nearly fifteen hundred feet (five hundred meters).

Facing Kingston across the harbor is a long, narrow spit of land called the Palisadoes. This is edged on the harbor side by the finest saltwater mangrove swamps in the Caribbean. It is not the mangrove swamps which bring the holiday-makers pouring along the Palisadoes, but the fact that at the end is one of Jamaica's most famous tourist attractions—the ancient town of Port Royal.

Port Royal was founded in the early seventeenth century. It offered good deepwater anchorage for ships and was heavily

44

fortified, having no less than one hundred and four guns. This particularly appealed to pirates—especially when they discovered that Port Royal also offered an excellent market for their booty, as well as plenty of entertainment. Then came the terrible earthquake of 1692. This was followed by an almost equally devastating fire twelve years later, and then a long series of hurricanes. As a result, by the beginning of this century Port Royal was just a tiny fishing village, almost completely ignored and forgotten, and only approachable by boat.

Then, in 1936, the Palisadoes Highway was constructed. In addition, the first of Jamaica's two international airports was opened just halfway along this new road. This immediately put Port Royal on the map again, and encouraged the construction of all kinds of

The Palisadoes, which face Kingston across the harbor. These are the finest salt-water mangrove swamps in the Caribbean.

tourist attractions, such as hotels, restaurants, a yacht harbor and even a large new lookout tower.

Port Royal also has one of the most fascinating small museums in the world. This contains all kinds of relics from old Port Royal, including cannons, bottles, pewter and silverware and a hoard of silver pieces of eight. But perhaps most touching of all is a brass watch, its hands still pointing to 11:39, exactly the moment disaster struck, one sunny summer morning over three hundred years ago.

6

Montego Bay and Other Towns

Montego Bay is the third largest town in Jamaica. It has a population of just over 40,000, and is growing very rapidly. It is also the center of the tourist trade, and is therefore the most cosmopolitan and least typically Jamaican of all the towns on the island.

The name "Montego" is said to come from the Spanish word for lard. Apparently, the Spaniards used the bay for shipping pork and beef fat back to Spain and to other parts of Europe. Most of the tourists call the town Mo' Bay, however, although no one seems to know why or when this practice first originated. One thing is certain, though, and that is that Montego Bay first became popular with tourists in the early years of this century. This was when a certain Dr. McCatty said that seawater bathing was good for the health. He set up a club at Montego Bay especially to encourage sea bathing, and from then on the town has been able to attract more and more wealthy visitors every year.

Today the most interesting part of the town is the seafront. It still

A view of Montego Bay, Jamaica's third largest town.

has many old wharves and warehouses, which are a reminder of the days when Montego Bay was just a port. There is also a "Cage" in the town square, which recalls something of the town's past. It dates from 1807, and used to be a jail for runaway slaves.

Spanish Town stands on the banks of the Cobre River. With a population of about 89,000 it is Jamaica's second largest town, but it still preserves much of its old historic charm. As Villa de la Vega, it was the island's capital for more than a hundred years under the Spaniards. It remained the capital for another two centuries under the British, although its name had by then been altered to Spanish Town.

Under the Spaniards, Spanish Town had two churches, an abbey and two monasteries. But when Oliver Cromwell's troops sacked the town in 1655, all these buildings were completely destroyed. An Anglican Cathedral was built on the site of one of the old Catholic churches, and a magnificent public square was built where the abbey and its surroundings had been. The most elegant new building of all was King's House, the residence of the British Governor-General. It was described at the time as "the noblest and best edifice of its kind anywhere, either in North America or in the West Indies." It was certainly the scene of a great many historic events, from a reception for Admiral Lord Nelson to the declaration of the abolition of slavery in Jamaica.

Despite all its prosperity, Spanish Town was gradually overtaken in size by Kingston. This was largely because the latter had a much better situation, with its large natural harbor. So, in 1872, the seat of government was transferred from Spanish Town to Kingston.

The "Cage," a jail that was used for runaway slaves dating from 1807 in Montego Bay's main square.

However, Spanish Town still attracts large numbers of tourists to look at its beautiful historic buildings.

Jamaica's fourth largest town is May Pen. On Fridays and Saturdays it is a seething mass of country people who have come to buy and sell at the market. They come by bus, car and cart, and even by train, as May Pen is a stop on Jamaica's only railroad line, which runs between Kingston and Montego Bay.

By far the highest town in Jamaica is Mandeville, situated at over

2,000 feet (nearly 700 meters) above sea level. In the past, it was very popular with British residents in Jamaica, who used to go there to enjoy the fresh breezes when it became too hot and sticky in Kingston or Spanish Town. Even today, Mandeville still has a slightly English appearance. There is a Georgian courthouse, an old stone church and the oldest golflinks on the island. A large number of Americans live there now, however, most of whom are connected with the nearby bauxite mine, or the factory where the bauxite is made into aluminum.

Port Antonio, in the east of the island, is a very attractive spot. It nestles between the mountains and a natural double harbor divided by the Titchfield Peninsula. At the end of the peninsula is Fort George. This has long since ceased to serve any military purpose but still has the remains of a wall ten feet (three meters) thick, and a number of cannons.

Port Antonio used to be a very popular place with tourists. But it was long ago overtaken by Montego Bay, although it is still a favorite resort for people who like to go deep-sea fishing. Port Antonio is also the principal port for the export of bananas, and the white banana boats can nearly always be seen either entering or leaving the harbor.

Savanna-la-Mar is a small town in the southwest of the island. It was founded in 1703, but it has been almost completely destroyed by hurricanes several times. For this reason, apart from the remains of a small fort, and one or two attractive old houses, it has little of historic interest. In fact, the most fascinating part of the town nowadays is undoubtedly the sugar wharf. Between mid-November

Port Antonio, a popular resort for deep-sea fishing enthusiasts.

and June, thousands of tons of sugar arrive there to be sent all over the world. As the harbor is not deep enough for large, oceangoing vessels, the sugar has to be tipped from the trucks into barges, which carry it out to ships lying about one mile (two kilometers) or so from the shore.

A much smaller town is Milk River Bath, the island's leading spa. According to legend, the healing properties of the water were discovered by a runaway slave, who found they healed his wounds after his master had beaten him. At any rate, the spring certainly has

52

the highest level of radioactivity of any mineral bath in the world, being fifty times higher than the spring at Vichy, in France.

Another interesting little town is Black River, which stands at the mouth of the river of the same name. This is Jamaica's longest river, although it is only about 44 miles (80 kilometers) in length. Black River has numerous quaint old houses, with fretwork balconies and shingled roofs, and some of them have upper stories projecting over the pavement, which shield the pedestrians from the sun.

7

The Rural Areas

Almost a third of Jamaica's population live in or around Kingston. What is more, the number of people leaving the country districts and moving into the capital is increasing every year. This may seem strange for a country which has an economy largely based on agriculture, but nowadays farming is becoming increasingly mechanized, and far fewer workers are needed on the land.

Nevertheless, the countryside is one of the loveliest features of Jamaica. There is a bewildering variety of scenery in a comparatively small area. Moreover, the weather is almost invariably inviting, except on the rare occasions when there is a hurricane. (There have been only nineteen hurricanes in the last one hundred years.)

The eastern end of the island is dominated by the great ridge of the Blue Mountains. These run southeast to west, with many spurs running to the north and the south. The mountains rise from sea level to over 7,500 feet (2,300 meters) in less than ten miles (eighteen kilometers), and are one of the most dramatic sights of their kind in the world.

Around the foothills of the Blue Mountains are numerous small holdings. These were originally the small plots of land given to the freed slaves in 1834. They are still cultivated in much the same way today as they were then; and most of the vegetables and fruit grown here are taken in brightly-colored trucks to be sold by the *higglers* in the markets in Kingston.

Further up the mountain there are several coffee factories. This is where the world-famous Blue Mountain coffee is produced. According to the experts, it is the exceptionally rich soil, combined with ideal climatic conditions, which make this coffee clearly superior to any other in the world.

Coffee production was at its height on the Blue Mountains in the early nineteenth century. But after the slaves were freed, the great plantations had to be divided up into much smaller plots of land. As a result, the amount of coffee produced dropped dramatically, and it is still only a fraction of what it was one hundred and fifty years or so ago.

The higher slopes of the Blue Mountains are covered with pines and other trees. There is also a profusion of ferns—some of which, called tree ferns, are no less than thirty feet (ten meters) tall. People often come up here to picnic, or even to stay the night in attractive log cabins, as there is a wonderful view, right over Kingston and out to sea.

Even higher up are the famous Cinchona Botanical Gardens. These cling to a ridge over 5,000 feet (about 1,600 meters) above sea

55

The Blue Mountains, where the world-famous coffee is produced.

level. They were founded in 1868, as a center for the cultivation of Assam tea and cinchona trees. (The bark of the cinchona tree was in great demand as a source of quinine, for treating malaria.) It later proved, however, that neither the tea nor the quinine could be produced economically, In fact, it was much cheaper to import both from India, where labor costs were considerably lower. So an Englishman took over the gardens to supply Kingston with vegetables and flowers. And today, as well as being a successful market garden, it is also a place of considerable interest for anyone who enjoys looking at plants.

The peak of the Blue Mountains is the highest point in Jamaica. There is no road to the top, and it can only be reached by a three-hour scramble up a rough track. Nevertheless, the view from the summit is breathtaking, and some people begin the ascent at two o'clock in the morning, especially to be at the top to see the dawn breaking.

To the east of the Blue Mountains there are a number of high limestone peaks. These are known as the John Crow Mountains. (John Crow is the Jamaican name for a vulture.) At the foot of these is one of the last Maroon settlements, called Moore Town, which like all the Maroon settlements held out against the British until as late as 1739.

Going west the land is still mountainous, but the mountains are much lower. Then, in the far west, there is the Cockpit Country. (Cockpit is the Jamaican word for a hole.) This is a curious area covered with thousands of small limestone potholes, hidden beneath dense bushes, and separated by narrow paths hardly wide enough to walk along in safety.

In the Cockpit Country is the largest settlement of Maroons on the island. Just as at Moore Town, the Maroons here are still ruled by a chief and his *osofu* (or council), and still retain their old tribal customs. Even now they pay no taxes and, if they commit any crime, except murder, they cannot be tried under Jamaican law, but only by other members of their own tribe.

In the south of the island, inland from Alligator Pond, it is very rocky and arid. This was one of the places where the Arawaks lived, and many of their artifacts and their rock carvings have been found in this area. There is also a very large limestone pit, about 160 feet (52 meters) deep, called God's Well, which contains very clear, turquoise-colored water.

Slightly further to the southwest is the largest swampy region in Jamaica. This area is known as the Great Morass, and its sides form a figure of eight around the Black River. This is where Jamaica's crocodiles mostly live, although there are not as many as there used to be, as large numbers have been killed, either for their skins or just for sport.

There are about one hundred and twenty other rivers, besides the

Cockpit Country

Black River, in Jamaica. In the north they are mostly narrow, tumbling streams, with numerous rapids and even small waterfalls. But in the south the rivers tend to be wider and not so fastflowing. In the summer, they usually dry up altogether, and there is nothing to see but a stony bed.

Visitors to Jamaica are often struck by the curious names of some of the districts and villages. There are, for instance, districts called the District of Look Behind, the Hellshire Hills and Me No Sen You No Come. And there are villages called Show Meself, Rat Trap, Wait-a-Bit, Bog Walk, Quick Step, Stonehenge, Tranquillity and, perhaps oddest of all, even Magotty!

8

Sugar and Other Agricultural Products

Sugar cane is a giant grass, about thirteen to sixteen feet (four to five meters) tall. It can be grown from seed, but the usual way of producing a new plant is to place a small cutting in the ground. This quickly grows roots and shoots to form a new clump of canes and, all being well, the canes should remain sturdy and healthy for the next six or seven years.

It is usually only some seven to eleven months after the cane has been planted that it reaches its full height. By this time the main stalk is about one inch (2.5 centimeters) in diameter. The sugar juice which the farmer wants is in the stalk. It is not in the leaves or in the roots under the ground.

Before the cane is cut, it is set on fire to burn off all the dry leaves. The stalk is extremely tough, however, and is not affected by the flames. Then the harvesting begins. This usually lasts from mid-November to June, but varies a little depending on how much rain there has been.

Sugarcane, a giant grass which grows to a height of 13 to 16 feet (4 to 5 meters) some seven to eleven months after planting.

Originally the canes were cut down by slaves, with huge knives known as machetes. But nowadays the cane is cut by machinery on nearly all the plantations. A kind of combine harvester cuts the cane close to the soil, chops it up into 20-inch (50-centimeter) lengths, and then transfers it to a truck which is driven along beside the harvester.

The cane arrives at the grinding mills either in trucks or by railroad. There it is squeezed between long, heavy rollers to extract all the juice. The juice is then clarified, to remove the impurities, and boiled until most of the liquid has been turned into brown crystals. This mixture then goes into a machine like an enormous spindryer. The drum of the dryer revolves at high speed and separates all the juice from the sugar crystals. It is in this raw form that the sugar is

61

Sugarcane stalks, harvested for processing.

usually exported to Europe and elsewhere, and the final refining, to turn it into the sugar the consumer buys, is normally done abroad.

There are many grinding mills in different parts of Jamaica. But the largest is at a place named Frome, about five miles (eight kilometers) north of Savanna-la-Mar. This one factory is capable of producing more than 10,000 tons of sugar every year. Most of the sugar from this factory is taken to the port of Savanna-la-Mar, and shipped overseas.

Nothing is wasted at a sugar mill. Even the fibrous matter called bagasse, which remains after the juice has been extracted from the sugarcane, can be used. It may be burnt in the factory to produce power, but it can also be sold to be made into such things as paper, rayon, nylon, animal foodstuff and fertilizers, and even into a kind of artificial wood.

The sugarcane industry also produces another extremely important by-product. This is molasses—a kind of dark brown syrup—which drains from the sugar during the course of manufacture. A small quantity of molasses is sold as black treacle, but a much larger quantity is exported, either to be made into cattle food or to be used in the manufacture of citric acid and vinegar. Some is used to grow special yeasts. These turn the sugar in the molasses into alcohol, which can be distilled to make rum. Jamaican rum is not only a very popular drink all over the world, but it can also be distilled yet again for use in the making of medicines.

Sugar and its by-products are no longer the main foreign currency earner for Jamaica. They have become steadily less important to the country's economy nowadays. This is due to competition from numerous other, much larger, sugarcane growing countries, such as Brazil, Cuba and India, all of which are producing several million tons of sugar every year.

Jamaica has various other agricultural products, some of which are exported. The most important are bananas, which were introduced into Jamaica by the Spaniards in about 1520. Other products include citrus fruits (which are chiefly grown around the Minho River), tobacco, coffee, cocoa, coconuts and ginger (which is mainly grown around Spaldings).

Metals have been mined in Jamaica ever since the days of the Spaniards. In fact, the Spaniards named one of Jamaica's rivers the Rio Cobre (the Copper River). But it was the discovery of large deposits of bauxite (the ore from which aluminum is made) a few

Helping with the rice harvest.

years ago that suddenly made mining a major industry on the island.

Bauxite can be found in more than a quarter of the island's surface. In fact, it is the red iron oxides in the bauxite which give the earth in Jamaica its typical red color. The bauxite is extracted from open-cast mines. These tend to disfigure the landscape, but can quite easily be filled in once the bauxite has been removed.

64

Today Jamaica is one of the world's largest producer of bauxite. Bauxite is the island's second most important foreign currency earner (after tourism). This is partly because all the mining is done by American firms, and most of the bauxite is exported in its raw form and reduced to aluminum in either the United States, Canada or Norway.

Gypsum is the main non-metallic mineral produced in Jamaica. The annual production is in the region of 200,000 tons. Approximately ten percent of this is used in the cement works in

Harvesting tobacco leaves.

Mining bauxite, the ore from which aluminum is made. Jamaica is the world's largest producer of bauxite.

Kingston. Most of the rest is exported to the United States, where it is generally made into plaster of paris.

There are numerous smaller industries in Jamaica, mainly in Kingston. These include various types of light engineering, tire manufacturing, and brewing. There is also an expanding food-processing industry, which means that the island's agricultural products can be canned or bottled before they are exported.

9

Family Life

The homes in which people live in Jamaica vary considerably. In the towns they may be anything from pleasant new bungalows to broken-down hovels. But in the country areas, most families live in the traditional Jamaican type of house. This may look rather ramshackle from the outside, but it is usually fairly comfortable.

The typical house is made of brightly painted wood. (Red and green are by far the most popular colors for houses in Jamaica.) It has a corrugated iron roof, which is usually also painted, and the whole house is generally raised a little off the ground on wooden piles so that the breeze can circulate all around it. In front of the house there is a big, shady veranda. This is where the family usually eat all their meals. Behind this are the kitchen, the living room and the bedrooms, all of which generally have old-fashioned sash windows, sometimes with wooden shutters to keep out the heat.

The inside walls of the house are generally painted some bright color. But the floors, which are also wood, are normally just stained.

The house is usually lit by electricity, and the cooking is done on an electric stove, although there are still a few families who are completely dependent on oil.

Outside the house there is always a coldwater tap. Even today, very few houses have any piped water inside. The Jamaicans accept this quite cheerfully, however, as only comparatively recently most families still had to collect all the water from a stream and carry it home.

Nearly every family in Jamaica has at least two, or even more, children, although in many of the poorer families the parents may not be formally married. This may seem surprising for a country where almost everyone professes some kind of religious belief, but the reasons behind it are largely historical.

In the days of slavery, the slave masters discouraged, or even actually forbade, their slaves to marry. So the slaves had little or no chance to have a wedding, even if they had wanted one. It is also the tradition in Jamaica that weddings should be highly elaborate, expensive affairs, with countless guests; and most Jamaicans seem to think that if they cannot afford a wedding of this kind then it is better not to have a wedding at all.

This does not mean, however, that family life is particularly unstable in Jamaica. In fact, in many cases children are brought up by both a father and a mother, just as if the parents were married. And even in the case of one-parent families, there are nearly always grandparents and countless other relatives to lend a hand, as most families are very tightly knit in Jamaica.

Among the better-off Jamaicans, the number of one-parent

68

A private nursery school. Although education is free in all state schools, a number of private fee-paying schools also exist.

families is probably no higher than anywhere else in the world. The children are also loved and spoiled a great deal—although probably no more than in the poor families, as Jamaicans of all classes will usually make almost any sacrifices for their children.

Since September 1973, education has been free in all state schools in Jamaica. (It had previously been free only for children in elementary schools, from the age of five to eleven.) But there are also quite a number of private fee-paying schools, varying from very expensive boarding establishments, run on English public school lines, to schools run by the Roman Catholic missions.

Officially, attendance at elementary school is compulsory. But, in fact, many children attend only very spasmodically, if at all—

particularly in country districts. One reason for this is that the parents often keep them at home to help in the house; another is that the parents sometimes cannot afford the compulsory school uniform.

The subjects studied at school in Jamaica are much the same as those studied anywhere else. The children begin by learning reading, writing and a little simple arithmetic. Their progress is often slow, however, especially in the village schools. More often than not, underpaid teachers have to try to cope with several large classes all crowded into one plain whitewashed room.

At the age of eleven, children can take a selection examination. This is to decide if they have the ability to go on to secondary education. Many children who might pass do not bother to try, however, as their parents want them to go to work, to bring some much-needed extra money into the family.

In fact, it is usually only the better-off children who go on to secondary school. There they find that the teaching is modelled very closely on the teaching in schools in Britain. English history, with emphasis on the development of the Commonwealth, and English literature are taught, as well as mathematics and science.

At the age of eighteen, some young people go on to further education. Jamaica has a college of arts, science and technology, a school of agriculture and no less than eleven teacher training colleges. The ambition of many young Jamaicans, however, is to go to the University of the West Indies, or U.W.I., as it is usually called, at Kingston. The university was founded in 1948, with only thirty-one students. But today it has more than 3,500, almost equally divided between men and women. It is also one of the most beautifully situated universities in the world, built on the site of several old sugar plantations, with old mills, storehouses and aqueducts still scattered among the new university buildings.

Although young Jamaicans are now being educated, there are still many illiterate adults. So the government has been making great efforts in recent years to teach them all to read and write. In addition, technical education and agricultural training are given to people who have had little or no schooling, to try to improve their chances of being able to obtain work.

Jamaican schoolgirls.

10

Food and Drink

People from all kinds of different backgrounds live in Jamaica—Europeans, Africans, Indians and Chinese. So it is hardly surprising that the food the Jamaicans eat, and the way it is prepared, varies widely—although certain dishes are eaten by almost everyone on the island.

One of the best-known meat dishes has the curious name of jerk pork. Small pieces of pork are covered with spices, and cooked slowly over a fire of green wood. The story goes that it was first eaten by the sailors who arrived with Columbus. They caught wild pigs and, as there was no dry firewood, they had to cook them over wood that was still green and wet. Another popular meat dish is known as pepperpot soup. In fact, it is a kind of stew, made of salt pork, salt beef and okra. Many Jamaicans also like curries, particularly curried goat, but visitors to the island often find the curries far too hot and spicy, compared with the curries they eat in their own countries.

The seas around Jamaica are teeming with fish. They are found in almost every size and variety, from huge sharks to sprats. Curiously enough, however, the Jamaicans do not eat as much fish as might be expected—probably because they prefer more highly flavored food.

The most popular fish dish is salt fish and *ackee*. This is boiled salted cod, served with a local fruit that tastes rather like scrambled eggs. This may sound odd, but ackee, which grows on tall trees and is poisonous until the fruit splits open, is in fact absolutely delicious when it is cooked. Other fish dishes include stuffed crabs. These are green land crabs, with the flesh chopped up and spiced, and served in their shells. Some people also like shrimps and lobsters, served in numerous different ways, mackerel (generally boiled in coconut milk) and spiced pickled herrings.

Green bananas, boiled or fried, are popular vegetables. So are boiled potatoes, yams and plantains (rather like large savory bananas). Breadfruit is also extremely popular, either boiled or fried. This is a round, green fruit, with a bumpy exterior, which tastes (not surprisingly) rather similar to bread.

One of the favorite desserts in Jamaica is grilled bananas. They are cooked in their skins, and served with a sauce made of a mixture of lime juice and rum. Some people are also fond of sweet-potato pudding, while others like guava cheese, a kind of thick, rubbery jelly, made by boiling strained guavas (yellow pear-shaped fruit) with sugar, and then letting the mixture set.

All the well-known fruits, like apples, oranges and bananas, are eaten in Jamaica. But there are other fruits, as well, which are not quite so common in other parts of the world. For example, there are

73

Bananas—one of the favorite fruits of Jamaicans.

mangoes, which have green skins and orange flesh surrounding a single large stone, avocado pears, pawpaws and limes.

For a snack the Jamaicans often have a meat pattie. This is a mixture of meat and breadcrumbs, with plenty of pepper, enclosed in a pastry case. People buy the patties at takeout cafés, or from stalls in the street, and can be seen walking along eating them at almost any time, from early morning to late at night.

The most famous Jamaican drink is, of course, rum. This has probably been produced in Jamaica for almost as long as sugarcane has been growing there. Rum was traditionally the drink of the

74

pirates who haunted the Caribbean. In fact, "Yo-ho-ho and a bottle of rum" is supposed to have been the pirates' favorite drinking song!

Today, most Jamaicans prefer a fairly light rum. This is quite different from the strong, dark drink which most rum-drinkers in Europe and America like. The Jamaicans usually mix the rum with ginger ale, or sometimes with coconut water (obtained from very young coconuts, before the liquid has become milky) or even with Coca-Cola.

As so many different fruits grow in Jamaica, there are naturally numerous fruit drinks. One of the most popular is made with a prickly green fruit called soursop, blended with milk. There is also

Bottling rum, the most famous Jamaican drink.

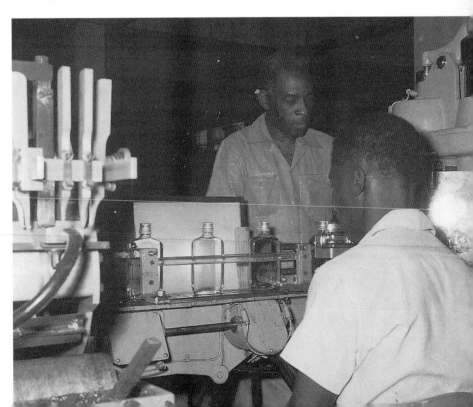

Picking mangoes, which make a popular thirst-quenching drink.

pawpaw nectar, mango nectar and tamarisk nectar, which are all exceptionally good for quenching the thirst when the weather is very hot. Coconut milk is also a very popular, cheap drink. In fact, stallholders in the street will just chop off the end of a coconut and hand it to the customer with a straw. Another cheap drink is sugar-cane juice, a sweet, greenish liquid, which is sold at street stalls, and is sometimes flavored by adding a little ginger.

One famous Jamaican drink is Blue Mountain coffee. The beans are grown on the plantations beside the small streams that run down the mountainside, and it is the most expensive coffee in the world.

In fact, it is much too dear for many ordinary Jamaicans to buy, but it is drunk by all the wealthier people on the island.

Fresh milk is very difficult to obtain in Jamaica, and most people seem quite happy to make do with either tinned or powdered milk. Many country people keep a few cows or goats, however, and give their children fresh milk to drink, as well as using it in cooking.

11

Sports and Pastimes

The Jamaican national game is without doubt cricket. When the West Indies are playing in a Test Match, everyday life comes almost to a standstill. Practically everyone is at home crouching over a radio (or, in the case of the better off, glued to the television set); and even the people who are still in the streets are holding transistors to their ears. There is naturally great rivalry among all the West Indian islands to get their players into the test team. But Jamaica usually manages to have two or three of its players selected. Despite this rivalry, cricket is almost certainly the greatest unifying factor (after the English language) among all the various countries which make up the former British West Indies.

Horseracing is also popular, although there is only one course in Jamaica. This is at Caymanas Park, about five and a half miles (nine kilometers) to the west of Kingston. There are races at least once a week, sometimes more, all through the year, but they are always flat races, with no hurdles or jumps. One reason why racing is so popular is that it offers Jamaicans one of the few

A Sunday afternoon cricket match. Cricket is by far the most popular sport in Jamaica and can be considered the national game.

opportunities they have to bet. (There are no casinos where people can gamble in Jamaica.) Also people enjoy going to the races because of the atmosphere on the course, which is rather like that of a fair, with steel bands, calypso dancing and a general air of festivity.

Soccer is quite popular in Jamaica, but there are no professional teams. The games that draw the biggest crowds are between the various high schools, which can sometimes produce some very exciting matches.

Easily the most popular indoor game among Jamaicans is dominoes. In fact, there can hardly be a man or a boy on the island who does not know how to play. The usual place for a game is the local "rum shop," where the players think out their moves while they sip the famous local drink.

One of the chief attractions of Jamaica for visitors is the glorious beaches which extend for more than 200 miles (320 kilometers) all around the island. What is more, apart from Doctor's Cave Beach at Montego Bay, which is always crowded, most of Jamaica's beautiful stretches of sand are very peaceful and quiet.

All the beaches slope gently, and are safe for swimming. The water is always delightfully warm, even when it is raining. Water skiing is popular, especially from the beach at Negril, as are windsurfing, scuba diving and, perhaps most exciting of all, skindiving among the beautiful coral reefs that are found all around the island.

Another popular sport is golf. There are eight 16-hole championship courses and one 9-hole course in Jamaica. Apart from the pleasure of the game itself, golfers can also enjoy the wonderful views of forests, mountains, streams and waterfalls that are so typical of Jamaica, as well as views of the beautiful, blue Caribbean.

Deep-sea fishing is excellent around the whole coast of Jamaica. Probably the best place to fish, however, is Port Antonio, where there is an annual international fishing tournament. The main catch for deep-sea fishermen are sailfish, blue marlin, dolphin, tuna and barracuda, although many other types of fish are quite often caught as well.

One of the best places for freshwater fishing is Black River. At one time it was also an excellent place for crocodile hunting, but this is now prohibited. Nearly all Jamaican streams and rivers provide very

Waterfall climbing at Dunn's River Falls.

good freshwater fishing, however, and such fish as bass and mullet abound in almost all of them.

A sport which is unique to Jamaica is waterfall climbing. The participants put on swimsuits and try to climb up to the top of the falls. There are several places where waterfall climbing is possible, but undoubtedly the best fun can be had at the famous Dunn's River Falls, which involves a climb of nearly 600 feet (200 meters).

Jamaica has plenty of caves for people who like to go exploring. The most easily accessible are the Nonsuch and the Runaway Bay

Caves, in the north of the island, which both have some remarkable stalagmites. For the more adventurous, however, there is the Windsor Cave, in the northeast, which is nearly 1fi miles (more than two kilometers) deep. There are no guides, however, so it is not suitable for anyone who is not experienced.

The most popular place for horseriding is Montego Bay, where riders can gallop for long distances along the sandy shore. Some people, however, prefer to hire a horse and trot gently through the sugar and banana plantations, and even along the winding tracks up the hills.

The Runaway Bay Caves.

Not strictly a sport, but very popular among the tourists, is rafting on the Rio Grande. This owes its origins to the days when bamboo rafts were used for transporting heavy goods down the river. The rafts are constructed of long bamboo rods, with a seat at the stern for two people, and an experienced local raftsman guides the raft with a low pole, from the front. Most people hire a raft at Berrydale, and go all the way to St. Margaret's Bay. This takes about two and a half hours, and includes stretches of calm water, but also some exciting rushing rapids. Some people even like to take a raft after dark, especially when there is a full moon, and glide gently down the river amid the mysterious tropical vegetation.

12

Arts, Crafts and Entertainment

Rather surprisingly, Jamaica has no long tradition of art, although in recent years great efforts have been made to encourage both painting and sculpture. The leading spirit behind this has undoubtedly been Edna Manley (the widow of one former prime minister and the mother of another), who was not only a talented sculptress herself but also one of the founders of the Jamaican School of Art. Manley was Jamaica's leading sculptor until her death in February 1987.

Although there is little native Jamaican art, the same is not true of crafts. But only a few of the crafts which depend on local materials are unique to the island. In most cases, the craft work in Jamaica is more or less the same as is found all over the Caribbean, with very little difference between one island and another.

One of the best Jamaican crafts is jewelry made from local semi-precious stones. These stones are only mined in Jamaica, mostly at the eastern end of the island. Expensive examples can be bought at

Wood-carving—a typically Jamaican craft.

all the smart boutiques, but less sophisticated versions are on sale in the government-sponsored craft markets, or even by the side of the road.

Another typically Jamaican craft are the beautiful wood-carvings made by the Rastafarians. Most of them are carved in *lignum vitae* ("the wood of life"), an attractive rose-colored local hardwood. These carvings vary from statues of all sizes to wooden masks, book ends, salad bowls, plates, cups and saucers and pineapple-shaped lamp-bases. Unfortunately there is also a considerable amount of greatly inferior wood carving on sale. (This is particularly true, of

A Jamaican wood-carving. The government is trying to raise the standard of all wood-carving to the highest possible level.

course, of the goods which are sold from the roadside stalls.) But recently the Jamaican government has been backing an educational program to try to raise the quality and standard of all local woodcarving to the highest possible level.

Objects made out of straw are also on sale all over Jamaica. But, apart from the belts and berets made by the Rastafarians, they are much the same as the straw goods sold anywhere else in the Caribbean. There are hats based on the type the slaves used to wear on the plantations, baskets, woven table- and beachmats, and anything else the shopkeepers think they can sell.

Furniture in Jamaica is also much the same as on any of the other Caribbean islands. Although it is often made out of the local mahogany, there is no particular local style. It is usually quite simply made, the chairs having seats and backs made of some woven material, with little or no decoration of any kind.

Entertainment in Jamaica is lively and quite plentiful. By far the most popular form is music. At one time, this usually meant whatever tunes and songs happened to be in fashion in Britain and America. There was also a rather despised local music, which can probably best be described as a bad imitation of the Trinidadian calypso.

Then suddenly, in 1962, a new kind of local music appeared. It was called *ska,* and had a very insistent beat, always accompanied by an arm-swinging dance. There were songs to it, as well, that

The Straw Market, Montego Bay. Straw goods such as these can be found all over the Caribbean and are not unique to Jamaica.

A memorial to the Rastafarian singer Bob Marley, who made reggae famous all over the world.

expressed a kind of social protest, and a sympathy for the frustrated young Jamaicans who could not get jobs, and were becoming dropouts from society.

It was from *ska* that steady rock and later the famous *reggae* developed. These were both somewhat similar to *ska*, but the singing and the music were more refined. *Reggae* was developed by the famous Rastafarian singer Bob Marley, and it was soon an easily recognizable form of music heard all over the world.

This does not mean that traditional local music has died out completely in Jamaica. In the villages where the Maroons live, for example, some very ancient forms of music and dancing still survive. People sit on the ground and beat out tunes on their drums, using their feet to alter the pitch, and dance much the same dances as their ancestors did long ago in West Africa.

There are several groups of performers who give excellent interpretations of Jamaican music and dance. Two of the best known are the Jamaica Folk Singers and the Jamaica National Dance Theater. To some extent their performances are arranged to suit foreign tourists, but by and large their work still retains a great deal of the vitality and the intensity which are so typical of the island.

Jamaica has two radio stations, broadcasting music, talks and news. In the evening, stations on other Caribbean islands, and even in the United States, can also be picked up. Jamaica has one television channel, but only the better-off people have sets at the moment. All broadcasting, both radio and television, used to be run by the government, however, freedom of the press now exists in Jamaica.

There are nearly thirty movie theaters in Jamaica, including several drive-in theaters. There are also several theaters, but they only have amateur performances, sometimes in one of the local dialects. The theater at Kingston puts on a traditional Christmas play every year. This is a great favorite with the children, and is always sold out.

Christmas is, of course, a holiday in Jamaica. In fact it is celebrated with a special kind of festivity called *Junkanoo*, all over the island. People wearing masks and fantastic costumes sing and dance in the streets of all the towns and villages, and everyone enjoys a great deal of feasting and rum-punch drinking.

Other traditional holidays in Jamaica are Boxing Day (the day after Christmas), New Year's Day, Ash Wednesday, Good Friday and Easter Monday. Then there is Labor Day in May, National Heroes' Day in October, and Jamaican Independence Day, with parades, music, dancing and an arts festival, on the first Monday in August.

13

Plants, Animals and Birds

When Columbus discovered Jamaica, the island was almost entirely covered with great forests. The only open spaces were a few clearings where the Arawaks had their small settlements. Virtually the only crops were cassava, arrowroot, maize and sweet potatoes, which the Arawaks had brought with them from South America.

The Spaniards cut down some of the trees and planted citrus fruits, sugarcane, bananas and coconuts. But it was the British who really cleared the forests, in the eighteenth and nineteenth centuries, in order to plant sugarcane and coffee. This resulted in a considerable amount of fine timber (mostly mahogany) suddenly becoming available. The mahogany was nearly all exported to England, where it was made into extremely high-quality furniture, by such famous craftsmen as Chippendale and Hepplewhite.

While most of the original trees were being cut down, a number of new ones were being introduced. These were nearly all trees bearing some kind of fruit which the new settlers thought they would like to eat. The most famous was the *ackee*, which was

An ackee tree. Ackee trees were brought to Jamaica from North Africa in the late eighteenth century.

brought to Jamaica from North Africa in about 1778, but mango and almond trees also arrived at about the same time. Another tree introduced at about this period was the breadfruit tree. Breadfruits were ordered by the slavemasters, who thought they would provide food for the slaves with the use of the least possible amount of land. The first breadfruit trees were brought from Tahiti by the famous Captain Bligh on the *Bounty* in 1793, and several of these sturdy original trees are still standing today, the largest ones being at Bluefields, in the southwest of the island.

Jamaica has more than three thousand different types of flowers. Of these, no less than eight hundred species are found nowhere else in the world. Apart from orchids, which grow profusely all over the island, the most common flowers include poinsettias, and poincianas, and vividly-colored hibiscus flowers, which are often as big as saucers.

The most numerous of the wild creatures in Jamaica are undoubtedly the bats. These are known locally as "rat-bats" to distinguish them from butterflies and moths, which are simply called "bats." There are at least twenty-five different species of rat-bats in Jamaica, mostly living in caves on fruit and insects—although one large rat-bat feeds on fish, and is often seen at dusk near the seashore.

Another very well-known animal in Jamaica is the mongoose. Oddly enough, the mongoose was only introduced in 1872, from India, to try to kill the rats which infested the sugar-cane fields. Previously boys had been employed to chase the rats, but without

Breadfruit. The first breadfruit trees were brought to Jamaica from Tahiti by the famous Captain Bligh on the *Bounty* in 1793.

An hibiscus flower—just one of the many species which grow in profusion all over Jamaica.

much success, and for a time it seemed that the mongoose was the perfect answer to keeping the rats under control. In fact, the mongooses did not take long to chase all the rats out of the sugar-cane fields. But the rats were not all killed, and a great many began damaging the coconut trees and the coffee plantations instead. What was worse, the mongoose itself soon became a pest, eating birds and lizards. In recent years, however, the government has managed to keep the mongoose population more or less under control.

In Jamaica, the crocodile is called an alligator. (Fortunately, there are no real alligators on the island, otherwise this might lead to confusion!) The crocodiles are quite numerous in the swamps along the south coast, some of them well over thirteen feet (four meters) long. There are none on the north coast—presumably because there are fewer swamps there.

Lizards of various types are quite commonplace in Jamaica. They are usually about 6-10 inches (15-25 centimeters) long, and some of the male lizards have a pretty fan round their throats. The only snakes which anyone is likely to see in Jamaica are harmless creatures more like worms than snakes, although there are a few constrictors of nine feet (three meters) or more in length, living deep in the forests.

Turtles can be found all around the Jamaican coast. In fact, in the seventeenth century no less than forty ships were engaged fulltime in catching them. Sailing ships returning to Europe would never have set out without a good supply of turtles, which would be killed during the journey to provide fresh meat for the sailors to help preserve their health and strength. The hawksbill turtle's shell is used to make so-called tortoise-shell eyeglass frames, handbag handles and so on, for export. In fact, turtles are so useful that there were once fears that they might become extinct, but the conservationists have recently managed to put these fears to rest.

Manatees (large aquatic mammals) can only be found along the south coast of Jamaica. (It was manatees that originally gave rise to all the various stories about mermaids.) Whales are also occasionally seen around the coast (there was once a small industry in catching and killing them), and several different types of porpoises are quite often observed.

The Jamaicans seem to have curiously little interest in birds. If they cannot eat them or put them in a cage, they just do not seem

A mongoose. Mongooses were originally introduced to Jamaica to control the rat population but soon became pests themselves.

to notice them. Nevertheless, there are at least twenty-five different types of birds which are found in Jamaica and in no other part of the world.

The daintiest and most fascinating birds in Jamaica must be the hummingbirds. The streamer-tail hummingbird (nicknamed the "doctor bird"), with its irridescent green breast, is found all over the island. So is the mango hummingbird, which is slightly larger, and looks rather drab until it takes to the air and opens its bright fanshaped tail. These two types of hummingbirds are found nowhere else but Jamaica. But a third type, the bee hummingbird,

96

is found on several Caribbean islands. It is only a little larger than a big bumblebee, and makes a beautiful cup-shaped nest.

There are two types of parrots in Jamaica, and also a parakeet. They are all bright green in color, with touches of red and blue here and there. Local people catch the parrots and sell them by the roadside. They are popular pets, as they can quite easily be taught to talk, and even to sing snatches of songs!

14

"Out of Many, One People"

Just after the Second World War, the British magazine *Punch* published a cartoon which showed some people standing in the rain in England, and looking longingly at a poster advertising holidays in sunny Jamaica. But it also showed a group of people in Jamaica looking equally eagerly at an advertisement offering jobs as bus conductors, railway workers, hospital domestic workers and so on in Britain.

This cartoon illustrates very vividly the position in Jamaica. It is a land of great beauty and natural riches, with a glorious sunny climate. For tourists who have money to spend it is a dream island, with long stretches of fine sandy beaches, and almost unlimited opportunity for virtually every kind of outdoor activity. But for the Jamaicans themselves, the position is very different. Thousands of them, in fact, leave the island every year to settle in Britain. The reason is that the cost of living is constantly going up, because so many goods have to be imported, including oil, steel, cars, most manufactured goods and even a great deal of food; and life for the poor is often a heartbreaking struggle.

Nevertheless, the position is slowly improving. After considerable government upheaval in the postwar years, the administration now appears at last to be reasonably stable. And at least Jamaica has no race or color problem. Unlike many parts of the world, there is equal opportunity for everyone, regardless of whether their skin is white, yellow, brown or black.

It is in fact, this feeling of unity that is Jamaica's greatest strength. This is probably best exemplified by the country's coat of arms, granted to the island in 1661. It shows two Arawaks, one on either side of a shield bearing five pineapples on a red cross, with a crocodile above the shield, and underneath Jamaica's motto—"Out of many, one people."

GLOSSARY

Arawaks	Native Indians of Jamaica.
bauxite	Ore that is the principle source of aluminum.
CARICOM	Caribbean Community and Common Market: a regional organization promoting trade within the region and abroad.
cricket	A game played with a ball and bat on eleven person teams with goals defended by batsmen considered to be Jamaica's national game.
Greater Antilles	Composed of Cuba, Hispaniola (Haiti and the Dominican Republic), Jamaica, Puerto Rico and the Cayman Islands.
higglers	Market women (hagglers).
Lesser Antilles	Composed of the Leeward Islands group, the Windward Islands group and the remaining Caribbean islands.
Maroons	Escaped slaves who lived in the mountains and forests of Jamaica. The Maroons resisted the British rule for many generations and finally made peace in 1739. Today the Maroons still retain many of their tribal customs and are ruled by tribal laws.

100

Patois	A language with different forms; a lyrical language dominated by English; used to describe dialects in the Caribbean.
Pocomania	A revivalist religious cult.
Rastafarian	Cultural religious group based on the belief that Ethiopian Emperor Haile Selassie was the reborn savior; movement originated in the 1930's, through the teachings of black nationalist Marcus Garvey.
reggae	Jamaican music form associated by choppy rhythms and politicized lyrics; popularized by Bob Marley and Rastafarianism.
ska	Jamaican music with an insistent beat accompanied by an arm-swinging dance.
West Indies	Group of islands comprising the Greater and Lesser Antilles; divides the Atlantic Ocean and the Cayman Islands.

INDEX

102